Animaths
Taking Away with Tigers

Tracey Steffora

Raintree

Raintree is an imprint of Capstone Global Library Limited, a company incorporated in England and Wales having its registered office at 7 Pilgrim Street, London, EC4V 6LB – Registered company number: 6695582

www.raintreepublishers.co.uk
myorders@raintreepublishers.co.uk

Text © Capstone Global Library Limited 2014
First published in hardback in 2014
First published in paperback in 2015

Edited by Daniel Nunn, Abby Colich, and Sian Smith
Designed by Joanna Hinton-Malivoire
Picture research by Elizabeth Alexander
Production by Victoria Fitzgerald
Originated by Capstone Global Library Ltd
Printed and bound in China by Leo Paper Products Ltd

ISBN 978 1 4062 6054 0 (hardback)
17 16 15 14 13
10 9 8 7 6 5 4 3 2 1

ISBN 978 1 4062 6061 8 (paperback)
18 17 16 15 14
10 9 8 7 6 5 4 3 2 1

British Library Cataloguing in Publication Data
A full catalogue record for this book is available from the British Library.

Acknowledgements
We would like to thank the following for permission to reproduce photographs: Shutterstock pp.4, 6, 8, 10, 11, 12, 14, 16, 17, 18 (© Eric Isselee), 5 (© Nick Biemans), 9 (© An Van de Wal), 17, 18 (© Iakov Filimonov), 20, 21 (© Volosina), 21 (© J. McPhail), 22 (© Cynthia Kidwell).

Front and back cover photographs of a white tiger reproduced with permission of Shutterstock (© Iakov Filimonov). Front cover photographs of Bengal tigers reproduced with permission of Shutterstock (© Eric Isselée).

We would like to thank Elaine Bennett for her invaluable help in the preparation of this book.

Every effort has been made to contact copyright holders of material reproduced in this book. Any omissions will be rectified in subsequent printings if notice is given to the publisher.

Contents

Some words are shown in bold, **like this**. You can find them in a glossary on page 23.

Taking away tigers

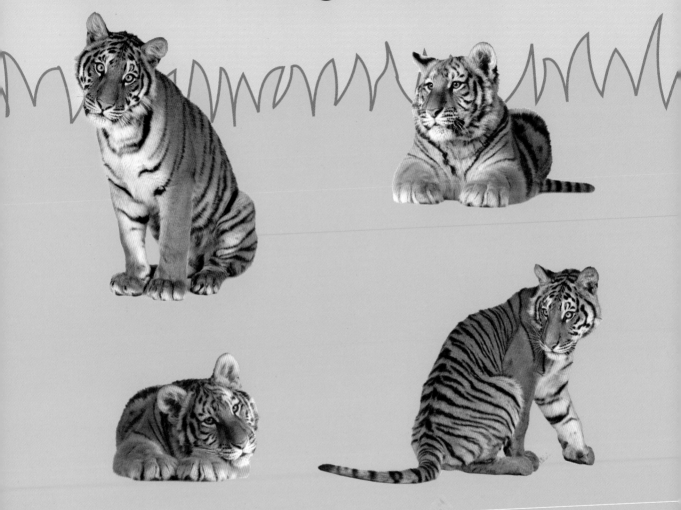

Look! There are four tigers in the jungle.

One tiger leaves and climbs a tree.
How many are left?

We take away to find out how many
are left.

Start with four.

Take one away.

Four take away one is three.

There are three tigers left.

When we take away something, we are **subtracting**.

$$4 - 1 = 3$$

Counting back

Here are the four tigers together again.

Now two tigers leave and go for a swim!
How many are left?

Subtract to find out how many are left.

We can count back to find out how many are left.

Start with four. Count back two.

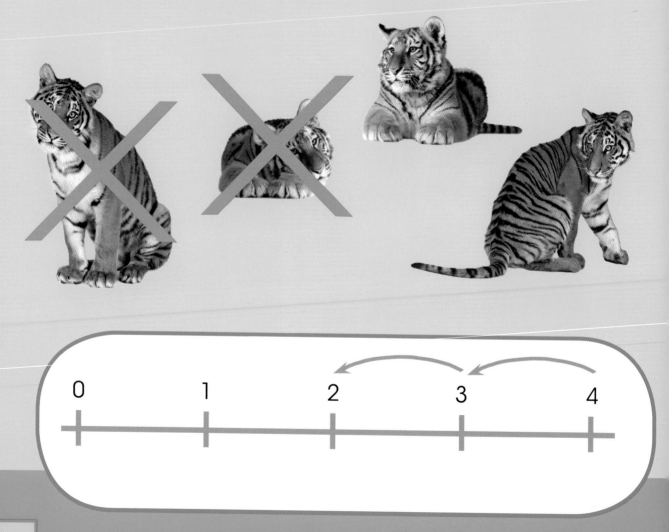

Four take away two **equals** two.

There are two tigers left.

Take away all

All four tigers are back in the jungle.

They all run off to hide.
How many are left?

Start with four. **Subtract** four.

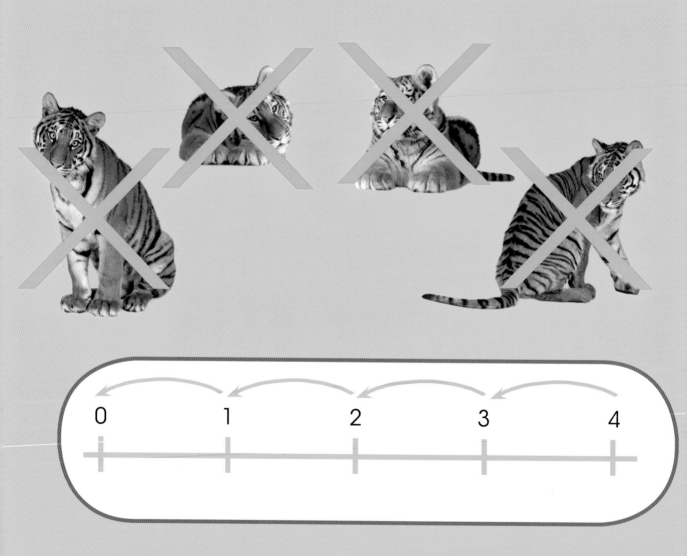

Four **minus** four is zero. Minus means something has been taken away. Zero means none or nothing.

There are no tigers left.

$$4 - 4 = 0$$

Comparing groups

Let's look at two groups of tigers. There are four orange Siberian tigers in this group.

There are three white Bengal tigers in this group.

How many more orange Siberian tigers are there?

We **subtract** to find out how many more.

Compare both groups of tigers. Take away the smaller number from the bigger number. This will tell you how many more orange Siberian tigers there are.

Four **minus** three is one. Minus is another way of saying take away.

There is one more orange Siberian tiger than white Bengal tiger.

How many are left?

Tigers like to eat meat! Here are five steaks.

A tiger eats three of the steaks. How many steaks are left?

5 − 3 = ?

Answer on page 22.

21

Tiger facts

- A group of tigers is called a streak.

- No two tigers have the same stripes.

- Tigers can leap up to about 9 metres!

- You can hear a tiger's roar from over 3 kilometres away!

- Tiger **cubs** stay with their mother for two or three years before living on their own.

Answer

page 21: There are two stacks left.

Maths glossary

compare look at two or more things to see how they are the same and how they are different

equals = This sign says equals. You use it to show the answer.

minus − This sign says minus. You use it to take away one number from another number.

subtract another way to say take away, or minus

Tiger glossary

cub the baby of a big cat, for example a young lion or a young tiger

Index